Original title:
Finding Meaning in a Cup of Tea

Copyright © 2025 Creative Arts Management OÜ
All rights reserved.

Author: Nora Sinclair
ISBN HARDBACK: 978-1-80566-174-0
ISBN PAPERBACK: 978-1-80566-469-7

The Essence of Calm

In every sip, a world appears,
A dance of flavors, calming fears.
The teabag's steeped, my worries flee,
Who knew this drink would set me free?

With friends we gather, cups in hand,
Laughter flows like grains of sand.
Watch tea leaves swirl, a swirling storm,
In porcelain boats, our hearts grow warm.

Brews of Insight

A pot of tea, a mind open wide,
Like magic potions, thoughts collide.
My mug keeps secrets, they softly spill,
With every sip, I find new thrills.

The kettle whistles, I start to think,
What life lessons lie at the brink?
My tea's a sage with leaves so wise,
Unraveling truths, to my surprise.

Steam Rising from Stillness

Steam curls gently, a fluffy friend,
In this warm embrace, I find my zen.
The chaos pauses, just for a sip,
A joyful jig, a tea-time trip.

The quirky cup, it seems to smile,
Inviting me to linger awhile.
So I raise it high, a silly cheer,
To the joys of tea and laughter near.

A Hug in Ceramic

Ceramic hugs for a heart so tired,
Steaming warmth, my soul inspired.
With every gulp, I feel so light,
A goofy grin, everything's right.

Tea leaves whisper, tales of fun,
In this cozy cup, I've already won.
So here's a toast, in playful glee,
To the humor found in my cup of tea!

Infusions of Introspection

In a world so vast and wide,
My teacup holds the truth inside.
I sip and ponder, it's quite the feat,
Is this chamomile or just my defeat?

Each swirl and swoosh, a thought will toss,
Why is my Earl Grey such a boss?
With every gulp of steaming brew,
I question life – what's wrong with you?

Liquid Comfort

A splash of milk in my favorite mug,
Is it comfort or just a warm hug?
Sipping slowly, I spy a cat,
Does he understand or just chase a rat?

Each teabag steeped with dreams galore,
What do I want? I'm not so sure.
But as I brew, my troubles cease,
With every sip, I taste my peace.

Leaves of Contemplation

In the kettle bubbles my grand design,
Should I add honey or let it dine?
Loose leaves whisper tales of yore,
Spilling secrets I can't ignore.

Dancing steam rises to greet my face,
Is life a puzzle or just a race?
As I ponder this over my pot,
I spill some tea—now that's my plot!

A Quiet Brew

In silence, I sip from my quaint little chair,
Does tea hold wisdom, or just tighten hair?
With each quiet slurp, the world's a stage,
I laugh at the thoughts of a wise old sage.

My cup overflows with questions big,
Like how many steeps make a mental jig?
Yet here I sip, in blissful delay,
Hoping to brew my worries away.

Tales from the Teapot

In the kettle, gossip swirls,
The leaves conspire, dance, and twirl.
Each sip, a story, steeped with glee,
Whispers of joy in my cup of spree.

The mug chuckles, warm in my hand,
Revealing secrets from far-off lands.
I raise it high, a toast to the brew,
Cheers to the par-tea, just me and you!

Chai and Contemplation

Chai brews deep, a fragrant quest,
In every sip, I try my best.
To ponder life, to question fate,
While dodging crumbs from the biscuit plate.

The sugar dances, a merry jig,
Spicing up thoughts, oh how they dig!
Do flies judge tea, or just think it sweet?
Philosophy sparked—thanks to my heat!

Elixirs of Existence

A splash of milk, a sprinkle of spice,
My potion brews, oh, isn't it nice?
As I sip, my woes take flight,
Who knew such magic hid in plain sight?

Laughter bubbles, a whimsical show,
Tea leaves chuckling, 'Oh, don't be slow!'
The world's vast problems seem less severe,
Each sip is wisdom, come, have a beer!

Layers of Aroma

The steam rises, like dreams to share,
With layers of scent that tickle the air.
A hint of jasmine, or maybe some mint?
The flavors tease out my inner flint.

As I ponder life—will it ever be clear?
My habits of brewing—why do I fear?
That maybe, just maybe, in each simple brew,
I find all the answers while sipping anew!

The Art of Steeping

In a saucer rests a dream,
Hot water's my bubbling stream.
Tea leaves swirl, a dance so grand,
Juggling fusion, oh so planned.

With a pinch of humor, steep away,
Life's troubles fade with each bouquet.
A teapot whispers, 'Why so blue?'
'Add some milk, and I'll cheer you!'

Meditative Brews

Brew a laugh with every sip,
Release your worries, let them slip.
Tea bags chuckle in the pot,
'Find your zen? Oh, why not!'

Lemon's sour, yet wise and bright,
Ginger giggles, brings delight.
As I ponder, steam takes flight,
A swirling visage, sheer delight.

Gentle Dialogue with Nature

Leaves murmur secrets in my cup,
Fermented tales of ups and downs.
Herbal friends with wisdom bold,
Share their laughs, but not the old.

'What's the fuss?' they seem to say,
'Just sip and savor your dismay!'
Nature's giggle coats the air,
In every brew, we share a dare.

The Dance of Steam

Amidst the steam, a ballet flows,
Tea and sugar strike a pose.
Ceramic twirls, a porcelain whirl,
As flavors clash, watch spirits swirl.

With a sip, the world's a stage,
Each cup uncorks another page.
Pour another round, let laughter rise,
In this teacup, see life's surprise!

The Comfort Cycle

In the morning glow, I brew a blend,
A swirling dance, my trusty friend.
With laughter bright and cookies near,
I sip away my morning fear.

Steam rises up, a gentle hug,
It quips and jokes, a cheeky mug.
Each sip a giggle, each gulp a cheer,
My worries vanish, they disappear.

Shadows in the Brew

A teacup sits with secrets deep,
In every swirl, a promise to keep.
Lurking shadows tease my mind,
What wisdom waits, what laughs to find?

The spoon it stirs, a dance so sly,
A splash of honey makes it fly.
With every sip, I'm lost in glee,
Who knew a cup could set me free?

Tasting the Moment

Brewed perfection in porcelain gleams,
Each sip is full of silly dreams.
I taste the moment, oh what a tease,
That ginger spice brings me to my knees.

Pouring forth a fragrant whiff,
I laugh out loud, it gives me a lift.
A dash of milk, a sprinkle of grin,
With every gulp, I giggle within.

Heat and Heart

Boiling water, a steamy twist,
That whistling kettle can't be missed.
I raise my cup with silly pride,
A brew of joy, that can't be denied.

In every sip, a punchline waits,
A tea party where fun creates.
Heat and heart, they swirl and play,
With each refreshing, bright bouquet.

Moments in a Teacup

In a cup of leaves, my thoughts take flight,
Bouncing like a ball, oh what a sight!
Sip by sip, I chase my dreams,
With every gulp, nothing's as it seems.

Laughter brews in boiling water,
A dance of flavors, oh how they chatter!
A splash of honey, a twirl of zest,
With every sip, I'm on a quest.

Steam and Serenity

Steam rises high, like a dragon's breath,
My worries dissolve, just like the rest.
Cup cuddled close, feels like a hug,
With each warm sip, I start to shrug.

The teabag's in, it's a wild affair,
Floating around, just like my hair!
I ponder life with a cheeky grin,
Tea leaves swirling, let the fun begin.

The Essence of Stillness

With a pinch of calm, I steep my bliss,
In this swirling cup, nothing amiss.
The world slows down, a joyful pause,
Even my cat gives a round of applause!

The porcelain throne holds tales untold,
Of crazy dreams and steamy bold.
Frothy whispers, they tickle my ear,
In this silent cup, my mind's a cheer!

Unearthing Flavorful Thoughts

From Earl Grey knights to chamomile queens,
In this tiny realm, I craft my scenes.
Tea leaves dance in a whirlpool spree,
Swirling boldly, just like me!

A splash of spice, a dash of play,
Each sip rewrites the rules of the day.
With lemon's grin and ginger's tease,
I find delight with every breeze!

A Dance with Dynamics

Boiling water, here we go,
Green or black, the choice is slow.
Stirring in flavors, a jolly spree,
Watch it swirl, my cup's a sea!

Lemon slices diving deep,
In a citrus' tango, I can't help but leap.
Add some sugar, watch it twirl,
With each sip, I'm in a whirl!

Aroma of Reflection

Steam wafts up, a fragrant tease,
Inhale deeply, oh what a breeze!
Thoughts awaken, dance in my brain,
Like little elves, they pop and regain!

Chai spices prance, laugh and tease,
Tickle my nose, oh, what a breeze!
Snickering flavors, take me far,
In this cup, I'm the star!

The Solace of Sip

Quiet time, my favorite game,
In my teacup, I'm never the same.
Giggling ghosts with every gulp,
Sip after sip, they make me jump!

Herbal hugs embrace my mind,
With each swish, new answers I find.
Laughter echoes in the leaves,
Who knew that comfort always achieves?

Tales in Teabags

In a teabag, stories reside,
Unfolding wisdom, brewed with pride.
Each steeping moment, a quirky chat,
My cup feels like a wise old bat!

Minty whispers, chamomile dreams,
Every sip, bursting at the seams.
Brewed adventures, some nonsense too,
In my mug, the world's askew!

Ceramics and Sentiments

In the kitchen, a clatter, all porcelain and clay,
My favorite mug is giggling, in a most foolish way.
It whispers to the Earl Grey, 'Let's steep for quite a while,

As our spoons dance a jig, with giggles and a smile.

Lemon slices in a ballet, a citrusy grand waltz,
The sugar cubes are headbanging, like they've got no faults.
They plop and swirl with laughter, as water begins to boil

Each sip a comedic skit, that's brewed in humble toil.

Threads of Tradition

Grandma's tea time secrets, tucked within a bag,
Each leaf a comic tale, each sip a silly brag.
She pours with such precision, a steamy comedy,
As I wait for the kettle, wearing my finest tee.

The strainer spins in circles, like a whirling dervish,
While biscuits join the fun, coated in a sherbet swish.
We share our treasured stories, over pastries piled high,
Plugging in our laughter, until the kettle's dry.

The Taste of Tranquility

A soothing cup of chaos, brewed to calm the storm,
The leaves chaotically swirling, in a most absurd form.
As I sip this potion, the world begins to fade,
Is it zen or giggles that this madness has conveyed?

The tea dances on my tongue, a waltz of sweet delight,
Like a jester in the castle, putting worries to flight.
With each fleeting moment, I smile at life's small jest,
Sipping on serenity, in a cup that feels like jest.

Essence of Togetherness

We gather at the table, all mugs lined up in a row,
Each one sportin' stories, and a comedic glow.
Chai and laughter mingle, steam rising in the air,
As friends crack goofy jokes, without a single care.

The cream swirls like a dancer, putting on a show,
While marshmallows float by like they're in a rowboat, slow.
With friendship as the base, we splash in silly cheer,
In our cups of warmth and joy, the world is always near.

Sip of Solitude

In a mug I sit, not a soul in sight,
With curls of steam, my pure delight.
A teabag plops, a splash of cheer,
I'm in my zone, no need for fear.

The cat is judging, as cats often do,
As I sip my brew, feeling brand new.
The world can spin, I won't engage,
I'll be right here, like a cozy sage.

The Comfort of Leaves

Each leaf's a tale, brewed warm and tight,
They whisper secrets, oh what a sight!
A dance of flavors, a whimsical show,
Like a comedy club, with lots of flow.

I clink my cup, a joyful chime,
Cheers to my steeps, it's tea time!
My friends are distant, but they're on my screen,
A virtual party, less awkward than it seems!

Infusions of Serenity

The kettle sings, quite the performer,
As I await my liquid warmer.
Hop, skip, a jump, to add some spice,
A sprinkle of laughter would be quite nice.

I taste the joy, it tickles my tongue,
In cups of wonder, a song is sung.
Forget the stress, let it steep away,
I'll giggle alone, all through the day.

A Steamy Revelation

A swirl of steam, like thoughts that play,
In every sip, I find a way.
With each hot gulp, a chuckle swells,
It's like a story, with tea it tells.

The flavor dances, a little wild,
A cup so funny, like a mischievous child.
So here's to the blends, both quirky and wise,
In every sip, a joyful surprise!

The Warm Embrace

In the morning sunlight, I brew,
A potion to wake me, it's true.
I spill a bit, oh what a sight,
The tea party ninja, still in fright!

Steam curls like whispers in the air,
My cat eyes it, with a daring stare.
One sip, and suddenly I'm wise,
Who knew breakfast could open our eyes?

A dance of leaves, with a splash of fun,
Who needs caffeine? Just gauge the pun!
With every drop, stories unfold,
Laughter brewed hot, never too cold!

So here's to the cup that warms my soul,
Where giggles and chuckles take a stroll.
Sip here, sip there, life is a game,
Tea in hand, we'll never be the same!

Rituals in the Rain

When raindrops tap in rhyming lines,
I grab my teapot, oh how it shines!
Dancing patterns, a silly parade,
With every splash, I'm serenely swayed.

Splashing outside becomes quite the show,
With tea in hand, I join in the flow.
A little drizzle, it softens my heart,
I sip and twirl, let the madness start!

I wear my raincoat, it's bright and wild,
Inside my cup, I'm a giggling child.
Each slurp is a jolt, like a jumpy spree,
Rainy day rituals? Just sip with glee!

With splashes and sips, the world feels light,
Drenched in laughter, everything's right.
So let it pour, let the locals see,
Dancing in puddles, just you wait for me!

Cozy Conversations

A quiet nook and a cup so round,
Where words flow freely, joy is found.
We spin tales of dragons and silly dreams,
Each sip a burst, or so it seems.

The magic brews with every pour,
We giggle at life, then come back for more.
Thoughts bouncing 'round like a crazy ball,
Tea's the magic, we're having a ball!

With a dash of honey, and a splash of play,
Conversations bubble, brightening the day.
Secrets exchanged with every hot sip,
Funny stories spill, making hearts skip!

In our cozy corner, we lighten the load,
With cups in hand, we dance on the road.
Laughter and tea, the best blend for me,
Oh, how delightful, this merry spree!

Brewing Connections

When water boils, it sings me a tune,
Bringing together, like sun and moon.
Friends gather round, the kettle on fire,
Our laughter brews higher and higher!

Each bag steeped in gossip and cheer,
With swirling aromas, we come near.
A pinch of humor, a splash of zest,
This cup of joy is simply the best!

Chai, green, or herbal; flavors collide,
With secrets spilled, we throw caution aside.
No one leaves thirsty, that's for sure,
In our teacup kingdom, we always endure!

So here's to the cup, the gathering place,
Where bonds are brewed with laughter and grace.
Clinks of our mugs, to the stories unfurled,
Tea time magic, let's conquer the world!

Calming Currents

In a mug of warmth, I see,
A tiny world, just for me.
Dancing leaves and swirling brew,
Who knew calm could taste like stew?

A spoon leaps in, doing a jig,
The teabag's got a wiggly gig.
Whispers rise from bubbling hot,
What's brewing here? A soothing plot!

Handle with care, it's boiling now,
Laughter steams up—don't ask me how!
Sip with joy, it's not too hot,
Every gulp's worth a silly thought!

Lost in flavors, sweet and bold,
In each cup, a tale unfolds.
Pour me two, I'll share the fun,
In tea time's game, we've all just won!

A Symphony of Sensations

Lift the cup to greet the day,
Notes of mint and honey play.
A symphony swirls in my head,
Who knew the kettle could be fed?

Bubbles burst like giggles bright,
Eager to join the morning light.
Each sip dances on my tongue,
A cheeky song just waiting to be sung.

Whisking whiskers and funny sounds,
Tea time joy knows no bounds.
Lifting spirits like it's a show,
With every taste, my worries go!

A sprinkle here, a dash of that,
Tea's got flair—imagine that!
Twirling flavors, let them blend,
In this brew, laughter won't end!

Stories in the Steam

Steam curls up like whispered tales,
Carrying secrets from leafy trails.
Brewed adventures in porcelain cups,
Where every sip just cheers me up!

A pinch of spice, a splash of cheer,
This magic potion brings good near.
Swirling clouds—the quiet might,
Revealing stories hidden from sight.

Floating thoughts in every rise,
Like goofy ghosts in good disguise.
Each drop a friend, a comical plot,
In liquid laughter, we're all caught!

A gentle nudge, that's how it goes,
In the warmth, my wit just flows.
So pour some joy, with a twist and turn,
Tea's own secrets, we wait to learn!

Each Sip a Secret

Every cup holds a tiny tale,
With quirks that'll make you turn pale.
Honey's giggle, the lemon's grin,
A brew so bright, it drowns the din.

Earl Grey whispers low and sweet,
Spilling laughter with every heat.
Sipping slow, it's my little cheat,
For moments filled with silly feat.

Tea leaves gossip, oh what fun,
They chat away till the day is done.
With every stir, a secret found,
In each cauldron, joy knows no bound.

Raise your cup filled to the brim,
Let's toast to life's delightful whim!
In every sip, there's laughter's grace,
Caught in tea's warm, silly embrace!

Sip, Breathe, Reflect

In a cozy nook, I take a seat,
With a steaming brew, life feels sweet.
I stir the thoughts with a clumsy hand,
Mirthful messes, oh, isn't it grand?

Sipping slowly, I spill some tea,
My cat looks on, amused to see.
The kettle whistles, what a delight,
Tea leaves dancing, oh what a sight!

Each sip a giggle, why so serious?
With a splash of honey, things get curious.
I ponder life but spill in style,
My little mess makes it all worthwhile!

So here's to tea, in good company,
A chuckle brews within its symmetry.
With silly sips and laughter broad,
I find joy in this moment, oh my, how odd!

Mugs and Memories

A mug so large, it winks at me,
Filled to the brim with wild jubilee.
I'd float away if I drank it all,
But who can resist such a caffeine ball?

Each sip recalls a wild escapade,
Like that time I thought I'd serenade.
With sugar spills and a swirl of cream,
My mug's a partner in every dream!

We've shared good laughs and bitter fights,
In its warm hug, I find delights.
Fragrant journeys in every drop,
This clumsy kettle can't make me stop!

So here's to my cup, my trusty mate,
Through all the moments, oh, isn't it great?
Together we sip, with laughter so free,
Each memory brewed, just my mug and me!

A Dance with Chai

The chai pot winks, it's time to dance,
With spices twirling, oh what a chance!
Ginger and cardamom feel so alive,
In this tea party, we all strive.

I clumsily pour, it splashes about,
The kitchen's a stage for a saucy shout!
Cinnamon sticks join in the fun,
In this frothy waltz, we're never done!

My taste buds tango, what a fine ride,
Giggling happily, they won't abide.
Each sip a kick, a playful tease,
This chai affair is sure to please!

So let's keep dancing, my spirited brew,
With sweet laughter, we'll see it through.
In this lively whirl, life's a charade,
With every cup, more joy is made!

Echoes of Elixirs

In the silence, a kettle hums,
Echoes of flavored joys as it comes.
A little splash, oh what a tease,
With whispers of laughter like a gentle breeze!

The first sip sings a playful note,
While crumbs from cookies swirl and float.
"Hey, did you taste that?" I shout with glee,
Each drop a story, come dance with me!

Pineapple vanilla or berry surprise,
Each blend's a poem under the skies.
So I sip and I chuckle, what's next to brew?
With tea's cheerful dance, there's always something new!

In every mug, a tale to tell,
Elixirs of life, they weave so well.
So join this chorus in a jovial spree,
With cups raised high, here's to jubilee!

Gradients of Grace

In a pot of boiling splendor,
Leaves dance like Williams at the end of a bender.
A splash of cream, oh what a sight,
No need for wine, it's pure delight.

Steeping wisdom in each swirl,
Forget the world, let laughter twirl.
With every sip, a joyful cheer,
Who knew such joy could come from here?

An artful mess upon the table,
A mystery brewed, as best as I'm able.
Patience tested as the kettle sings,
In the city of mugs, I'm the king of blings.

A dance of flavors, a bubbling tease,
In this frothy world, I find my ease.
From chai to green, a merry feast,
I toast to tea, my joyful beast!

Comfort in a China Cup

I clink my cup, it's porcelain grace,
A cozy hug, a warm embrace.
Tea leaves whisper, secrets profound,
In my china friend, solace is found.

One sip and I'm off on a quest,
Adventures brewing, life at its best.
Laughter bubbles, it's quite absurd,
Tea's got wisdom, and so does a bird!

Lemon and honey, a zesty pair,
Make dull moments jump, with flair!
Pouring joy, a comedic show,
In a china cup, my worries flow.

So here's to the laughter that tea can create,
With each bubbling joke, it's never too late.
Raise your cups, let the clatter proclaim,
Tea is the secret, and joy is the game!

Reverie in Ritual

Morning ritual, my quirky affair,
Loose leaves tangled, but I don't care.
Kettle whistles, what a funny sound,
Each little bubble, joy unbound.

Steep for a moment, then rescue the lace,
Tea time dances with an elegant grace.
Forget the rush, it's a silly spree,
In my cup, I'm as bright as can be!

Friends may wander, but tea stays true,
Fleeting moments, joys to pursue.
In porcelain gardens, we swan and swap,
Laughter sprinkles, tea never stops!

A splash of whimsy, a twist of fate,
In the tea leaves, I contemplate.
Pour another round, laughter rings clear,
In this ritual, my heart draws near.

Mellow Moments

Mellow moods drift as tea brews slow,
In my comfy chair, I steal the show.
Biscuit crumbs dance with a jiggle and spin,
Each sip and nibble, a delighted grin.

Sipping stories, both old and new,
In this tea party, I'm quite the crew.
A dash of jam, a dollop of glee,
In my little teacup, there's magic, you see!

Caffeine dreams and playful schemes,
Brewed mischief captured in my beams.
Sloshing joy, what a whimsical plight,
A tea-time delight that feels just right!

So here's to the giggles and hilarious spills,
With each delightful cup, I cure all ills.
Raise your mugs, let the laughter decree,
In these mellow moments, just let it be!

Journeys in a Teabowl

A whirl of leaves in swirls of steam,
I travel far within this dream.
Each sip I take, a tale unfolds,
Of daring knights and dragons bold.

The biscuit crumbles, oh what fun,
Waves of laughter, the game begun.
With every brew, my cares dissolve,
In tea we trust, our problems solve.

The kettle sings a joyful tune,
With every pour, I feel immune.
Brewed wonders in a simple cup,
Life's riddles seem to bubble up.

So let us sip and share a grin,
For every cup, a new begin.
In this teabowl, we'll take our flight,
To lands of whimsy, pure delight.

Warmth in the Ordinary

On dreary days, when skies are grey,
A mug of joy will save the day.
With quirky mugs and spoons that dance,
Each sip a spark, a joyful chance.

Steam rises like a playful sprite,
A swirling hug, oh what a sight!
Life's monotony fades away,
With every drop, I laugh and sway.

My cat joins in, with prying paws,
As tea flows forth, I feel applause.
In this hot brew, the odd reveals,
The warmth of life, it gently heals.

So pour another, don't hold back,
With every fill, I'm on the track.
In common moments, joy is found,
In simple sips, we gather round.

A Cup of Clarity

In tepid waters, wisdom stirs,
With sips of spice, the fog blurs.
Conundrums float on leaves of green,
Each brew a laugh, a thought unseen.

The fragrant dance, a swirling cheer,
Silly musings, loud and clear.
I ponder life with every brew,
What's real, what's tea, and who's the fool?

The leaves may curl, yet thoughts unfurl,
My mind's in motion, what a whirl!
Cup in hand, I chase my muse,
Curious blends, I cannot refuse.

With every gulp, new visions rise,
A twist of fate in tea disguise.
So laugh with me, let's spill the beans,
In this cup of clarity, we're queens!

Brewed Tranquility

In porcelain peace, I find my place,
A dance of flavors, a warm embrace.
With every sip, the world slows down,
In this little cup, I wear my crown.

The world outside may rush and race,
But here I dwell, a slower pace.
With jasmine whispers and minty dreams,
I float away on fragrant streams.

The steaming brew, an alchemist's art,
Turns hectic days to calm and smart.
Each drop a giggle, a tiny cheer,
In this brewed bliss, I shed my fear.

So let us toast to cups of love,
To treasures found in warmth thereof.
In every sip, a wink, a smile,
Brewed tranquility, my heart's the style.

Chasing Shadows in the Brew

In the swirl of my cup, a tale does unfold,
Laughter dances like steam, oh so bold.
I stir and I ponder, where does it lead?
Perhaps to a fortune, or just more of mead.

The leaves spin their yarns, in a twist and a turn,
Whispering secrets, as I sip and I yearn.
Every sip a riddle, a puzzle so sly,
Is it magic, or just tea leaves that lie?

With a grin I observe, the bottom of the mug,
Is it wisdom I see, or just a wet rug?
Oh, the tales that they tell, with every steeped glance,
A comedy brewing, oh what a romance!

So here's to the laughter, in every hot drop,
A whimsical journey that never will stop.
In the shadows of brews, one finds what it means,
To laugh through the flavors, in life's silly scenes.

Heart and Hearth

A kettle sings sweetly, its song full of cheer,
Bubbles bursting like jokes, filling hearts near.
In cups of bright porcelain, smiles bloom and grow,
The laughter around the table, oh how it flows!

We brew up mischief with the sugar and spice,
A pinch of the giggles, and all feels so nice.
Each sip a reminder, of moments we share,
In the heart of the hearth, there's love everywhere.

Watch as the leaves take a twist and a dive,
Like stories that dance, keeping memories alive.
With each little slurp, we toast to the fun,
As we sit and we sip, till the day's nearly done.

So let's hoist our mugs, full of laughter and glee,
In the warmth of this kitchen, it's just you and me.
For every hot cup brings unity's glow,
In moments together, oh how true joy can flow!

The Soul of Steeping

Oh, the leaves take a plunge, splashing thoughts like a game,
Giving zest to my afternoon in a beauty untame.
With giggles and sighs, I soak in the strife,
A steamy relation, my cup and my life.

In the depths of my brew, a mystery lies,
Like a puzzle of socks that got lost in the guise.
I sip and I muse, is it tea or a spell?
For each hearty swallow, I tumble and dwell.

With friends by my side, we'll spin tales 'till late,
As the droplets join in, weaving laughter from fate.
Each bubble a blessing, a minute to keep,
As the warmth of our laughter keeps us from sleep.

Steeping secrets and giggles in tones oh so bright,
With a dance in my cup, I find joy in the night.
For in every calm sip, there's a hint of delight,
As we sip and we chuckle, till morning's first light.

Reflections of Light

In the depths of my tea, reflections abound,
A kaleidoscope world where humor is found.
The sunlight peeks in, a painter so sly,
Turning water to gold, oh, my how they fly!

Each leaf twirls with glee in a watery dance,
They're here for the laughter, not leaving to chance.
With every warm sip, a grin finds its place,
As I dive through this journey, the troubles erase.

Like a jester's bright hat, with colors galore,
The tea shares a joke, I'm left wanting more!
The folly of life is steeped with delight,
In each cozy moment, it feels oh-so right.

So come raise your cup, let's celebrate we,
The joyful reflections in our cup of tea.
With laughter and warmth, our spirits aflame,
In this beautiful dance, we'll never be the same!

Sips of Wisdom

A tea bag floats like my thoughts,
In a pot as old as time.
I ponder life while it steeps,
Wondering if I'll rhyme.

The kettle sings, it's like a song,
It makes my worries flee.
I stir it well, but who's to say,
If it's wise or just my tea?

Each sip reveals a mystery,
Of flavors bold and bright.
Yet with one sugar, all is clear,
As sweetness tastes just right.

The leaves dance in the bottom,
A waltz of leaf and steam.
Who knew old bags had secrets,
That laugh at life's grand scheme?

Moments in a Mug

My mug is full of mischief,
With spills and frothy foam.
Each gulp a giggling hiccup,
That makes me feel at home.

Every dunk of biscuit,
Is a moment to embrace.
Crunchy joy collides with tea,
In a delicious race.

The teapot's funny face,
Looks back with knowing eyes.
"What is your grand life lesson?"
I smile, "It's just a prize!"

In every warm reflection,
I find a silly cheer.
With each sip, the world spins 'round,
And laughter's what I hear.

Leaves of Life

The leaves whisper secrets,
Of mornings long and bright.
They giggle in the pot,
As they twirl with pure delight.

A dash of mint and lemon,
Turns my frown upside down.
With every twist and turn,
I'm glad I wore this crown.

They say tea holds wisdom,
But I think it's just a ruse.
It's simply hot and steamy,
With flavors I can't refuse.

So cheers to leafy laughter,
In pots both big and small.
For every sip we take, my friend,
Brings joy to one and all.

Liquid Reflection

In a cup of liquid dreams,
I stare and lose my way.
It's either tea or goldfish,
That brighten up my day.

The steam writes silly stories,
In letters bold and clear.
I laugh and sip, it's magic,
With a hint of ginger cheer.

Each swirl tells a joke,
With humor hot and bright.
Mixing folly with the leaves,
Oh what a funny sight!

So here's to liquid laughter,
In every single swig.
May your cup always brim full,
With joy that's pretty big.

The Language of Leaves

In the bottom of my cup, a riddle lies,
Tea leaves twist, dance, and disguise.
They speak in whispers, oh what a thrill,
I ponder their secrets, then spill them still.

A fortune told in chamomile blooms,
Of cats wearing hats and confused brooms.
I clutch my mug, it chuckles back,
Life's quirks brewed up in this cozy shack.

With every sip, I swear I see,
A dance-off brewing between my tea and me.
The Earl Grey grins with a zesty flair,
While sleepy green rolls with tousled hair.

So here I sit, my cup afloat,
With silly thoughts, let me emote.
For in these leaves, I find delight,
A cup of laughter, morning to night.

Notes of Nostalgia

The kettle whistles, a sweet refrain,
A symphony of memories, not quite sane.
Each splash of tea like echoes of yore,
Mismatched socks and tales galore.

Grandma's laughter, a pinch of spice,
Teaspoons of sugar, oh so nice.
A ginger-infused trip down memory lane,
Where socks are lost, but joy remains.

I clink my cup like a castanet,
Reminiscing on the last time I met.
Friends chatting over lemon's zest,
As time was lost in the teacup's nest.

So here's to those notes from yesterday's brew,
A laugh, a smile, a warm déjà vu.
For every drop carries a sweet refrain,
In the melody of life, let's sip again.

Teardrops in Tea

When my tea spills, oh what a mess,
A puddle of feelings, I must confess.
Each droplet a story, a tale to tell,
Of late-night snacks and hiccups as well.

It's a splash of joy, a sprinkle of woe,
Yesterday's dramas in each brew's flow.
With laughter through tears, I take a sip,
A teardrop turned joy, a wobbly trip.

That lemon twist is downright cheeky,
As I ponder life's quirks, oh so sneaky.
Tea's playful nature makes my heart sing,
Like a jester who dances on a colorful wing.

So raise your cup to spills and glee,
To teardrops in tea, and silly esprit.
For life's perfect brew is laughter and cheer,
A splash of chaos, let's raise it near.

Aromatic Anchors

An anchor of spice in my favorite mug,
A swirl of aromas that gives me a hug.
Minty whispers and chai's warm grin,
   I savor each sip like a gentle win.

Scented treasures like a fragrant tease,
Flowing like stories across soft breeze.
The cinnamon winks, the cardamom sighs,
   A narrative unfolds with every surprise.

Oh, the dance of flavors that tickle my nose,
A carnival of taste, where silliness grows.
With each little sip, I find my delight,
In the sweet-smelling chaos, laughter takes flight.

So here's to the anchors brewed with charm,
   To a cup that wraps me in savory calm.
   For in these aromas, life's humor hides,
   In every spiced sip, the laughter abides.

Sips of Solitude

In a mug so wide, I seek my fate,
Tea leaves dance, it seems they wait.
With every sip, a smile breaks free,
Contemplating life's sweet irony.

A splash of milk, a twist of fate,
Stirring thoughts, I contemplate.
Why did I think I could be profound,
With a teabag's wisdom swirling around?

The kettle sings, a cheerful tune,
Whispers of nonsense, I hear them croon.
As I ponder this world so vast,
My tea grows cold, the moments pass.

A cookie joins, a friendly face,
In this warm cup, there's no disgrace.
With each delightful, silly sip,
I savor life, and let it rip!

Whispers in Warmth

Steaming secrets brew in my cup,
Each sip dances, filling me up.
Life's absurdities, oh how they flow,
In this cozy warmth, I'd like to grow.

Laughter brews with every steep,
With my tea, I take a leap.
Dunking biscuits, crumbs on my face,
In this delightful, chaotic space.

Sipping slowly, a sip to savor,
Finding joy in every flavor.
A teapot's tales, so rich and bright,
Emerge like shadows in morning light.

With a giggle, I clink my cup,
What a way to cheer me up!
In this whirlpool of warmth and cheer,
I find my bliss; my soul draws near!

Brewed Reflections

In the depths of this porcelain lake,
Thoughts drift and swirl, oh for goodness' sake!
Why did I choose this blends and brews?
As I sip away, I find my muse.

With chamomile dreams and green tea tales,
A hint of madness, the love prevails.
The kettle's whistle, a siren's call,
Rising to greet me, I can't stall.

Through swirling steam, I ponder life's game,
Is it just me, or is it all the same?
A dash of honey, sweetened surprise,
In the chaos, I find my replies.

While the world spins on, I sit and sip,
In this cup, life's meaning takes a trip.
Crack a joke or two, let giggles flow,
In a sunset's shimmer, I savor slow.

The Art of Steeping Silence

In this quiet corner, my cup resides,
A sanctuary where silliness hides.
With a single bag, the magic starts,
Steeping peace in silly parts.

As scent wraps around, I question fate,
Did I really need all this debate?
Tea leaves whisper jokes in my ear,
During moments of silence, I hold dear.

With each slurp, I'm lost in thought,
Is this the meaning that I sought?
The more I sip, the less I know,
As giggles erupt in a steady flow.

The bottom's near, a reflection clear,
Laughter and warmth, my path so dear.
So cheers to the drink, that solves it all,
In my quiet cup, I heed the call!

The Stillness Within

In a world that spins so fast,
My teacup holds a moment's cast.
With steam that swirls like dance divine,
I ponder life, and sip the brine.

The pot, it whistles, quite a song,
While I decide what feels right, wrong.
Do I want a dash of spice?
Or green so bland, it won't entice?

One cup makes depth, one cup makes light,
Each sip is a chance, a delight.
Like kids in rain, we frolic in tea,
Pouring feelings as wild as can be.

So here I sit with cup in hand,
Concocting dreams and tea so grand.
Laughter brews within the cup,
A toast to life, I drink it up!

Fragrant Destinations

Each leaf a ticket, each sip a ride,
To lands of ginger and matcha pride.
With tea I've traveled far and wide,
To places where flavors abide.

Earl Grey sirens sing my name,
While chamomile whispers of sweet, sweet fame.
A cinnamon forest, oh what a sight,
In my cup, stars twinkling at night.

The French toast tea is quite a tease,
I chuckle as it dances with ease.
When friends are near, oh how we laugh,
Over bubbles and brews, our silly craft.

Each sip a joke, a light-hearted jest,
In the world of tea, we're truly blessed.
We brew our mischief, steep our fun,
With every cup, another pun!

Rooted in Ritual

Every morning, ritual frames,
Tap the kettle and call its names.
The dance of tea in swirling brew,
A waltz of flavors, nothing new!

I'm sure my cup judges my whims,
As I ponder if it's tea time hymns.
Do I sweeten with honey or tart with lime?
Oh, decisions, decisions—anti-crime!

The biscuit dips, a joyous splash,
In hot embrace, oh what a clash!
We giggle as the crumbs find home,
A tea party in my mind, I roam.

Each brew a lesson, a merry muse,
With flavors that light my chosen fuse.
So, here's to cups, both tall and stout,
In sips of joy, we sing and shout!

Clarity in Clarity

Amidst the chaos, I find my peace,
In muddy cups, my thoughts release.
Clear as the tea I steep for fun,
What's brewed within? A clever pun!

With every pour, my doubts lose weight,
I brew my plans and contemplate.
Should I add a splash or leave it be?
The cup, my friend, knows best for me.

A sip of calm, a cheeky grin,
With every stir, new worlds begin.
Laughter floats upon the steam,
In the land of tea, we dare to dream.

With flavors bold, and stories shared,
I'll spill my heart, I'm never scared.
So raise your cup, let's have a laugh,
In clarity, let's do the math!

Essence of the Everyday

Pouring hot water, it's a miracle,
Leaves dance like they've lost control.
A sip reveals secrets, a laugh in the steam,
Who knew a teacup could hold a dream?

Stirring in sugar, a sweet little joke,
The kettle whistles, it surely can poke.
Friends gather 'round, no need for a spree,
Just add laughter to that cup of glee.

Life's swirling flavors, no recipe guide,
Each steep brings a giggle, what fun to abide!
Brewed liquid joy, with a hint of surprise,
In this tea party, we win the prize!

So raise up your cups, here's to the bliss,
Hot tea in hand, I wouldn't miss.
A sip of the ordinary turns silly and bright,
In the world of a teacup, the laughter takes flight.

Savoring Simplicity

In a porcelain world, there's calm in the brew,
Each cup holds a tale—just me and my crew.
Boiling away worries, that's how it's done,
With every warm sip, I laugh just for fun.

A pinch of this, a dash of that,
Steeping imperfections, imagine that!
It's just hot water, or so it would seem,
But it's magic revealed in every sweet dream.

Teabags doing the cha-cha in the pot,
Life has its humor, and this is the plot!
Nothing quite fancy, no need to impress,
Just a cup of contentment; who needs the rest?

So let's clink our mugs, a toast to the day,
In the simplest of moments, let laughter stay.
Sip by sip, our troubles take flight,
In a world full of tea, everything feels right.

Zen in the Teacup

In the depths of my teacup, a universe swirls,
With leaves like philosophers, ending in twirls.
They ponder the cosmos, while I take a sip,
A zen moment found, yet I spill it—oh flip!

With a giggle and spill, life's lessons unfold,
In the dance of the droplets, each story retold.
Tea time's a canvas, where humor will sprout,
With flavors of joy, there's no room for doubt.

I take a deep breath; let the aromas just cling,
A laugh bubbling up, this simple little thing.
A splash of calm, with a side of delight,
'Zen' may be tricky, but this feels quite right!

So raise your steeped cups as we share this embrace,
In the laughter and warmth, let's find our own space.
Sipping together, we are bold and carefree,
In the zen of our cups, we laugh joyfully.

Harbors of Hot Water

A kettle's serenade starts the day anew,
Bubbles of laughter cheerfully brew.
The teacups all gather, a quirky brigade,
In harbors of hot water, our worries cascade.

Leaves positively gossip as they steep with delight,
Exchanging their secrets till the color's just right.
Stirring up flavors, we're playful and spry,
Caffeine and chuckles—let time flutter by!

Every drop is a treasure, every sip a delight,
We toast to simplicity, from morning till night.
With each swirling whirlpool, we find joy in the flow,
Tea is our compass; together we go!

So here's to the moments spent steeping away,
In harbors of hot water, we laugh and we play.
A cup full of mirth in this sweet little scene,
With friendships that steep, it's the best kind of tea!

Brewed Wisdom

In a mug of steaming delight,
Sits wisdom, cozy, not too tight.
Each sip, a giggle, a gentle nudge,
Life's biggest questions—let's not judge.

With leaves that dance and twirl with glee,
They whisper, 'Why not just be free?'
A splash of milk, a sugar tease,
Philosophy brewed, oh what a breeze!

The kettle sings with a joyful tune,
Brewing truth like a cartoon spoon.
Sip by sip, the world feels bright,
In this cup, I find my light.

So raise your mug, and don't you fret,
In every gulp, there's more to get.
Life's a blend, both bitter and sweet,
Trust the tea, it can't be beat!

Flavors of Self-Discovery

In the cup, mashed hopes collide,
Peach or lemon, what's inside?
Each flavor tells a quirky tale,
Of days gone past and friends so pale.

Oh, a hint of mint, like a silly friend,
Who cracks a joke and won't rescind.
While chocolates swirl, with a wink so sly,
They say, 'Eat dessert before you die!'

The tea leaves twist, spinning profound,
In a world where laughter's always found.
Sip with zest, and spill some sass,
Life's too short for boring glass!

So let the flavors dance and cheer,
In every sip, draw friends near.
With each taste of joy, so absurd and grand,
Discover yourself in every strand!

Whispers of Warmth

A cup of warmth in the morning light,
Whispers softly, 'Don't take flight.'
With honey drizzles and giggles too,
It's hard to be mad when you've got a brew.

The steam rises, like dreams afloat,
"Is this my life?" I giddily gloat.
Through chamomile blooms, soft stories arise,
Oh, this tea knows all my sighs!

Sipping slow, I peek inside,
At frothy joys I can't abide.
With a splash of whimsy, I tune in tight,
Finding comfort in every bite.

So gather 'round, for a silly tea spree,
Who knew that mischief could taste so free?
With friends aplenty, let's share a laugh,
In this bubbling bowl of heart's warm path!

Brewed Reflections

In the depths of a steaming brew,
I see reflections, oh so true.
Glimmers of joy, hints of despair,
All float gently in the air.

With every sip, a chuckle sneaks,
As bittersweet moments play hide and seek.
A splash of drama, a dash of fun,
The kettle knows how it's all done!

Lemon zings in a cheeky way,
As I ponder what to do today.
Should I dance, or take a nap?
The tea just giggles—what a trap!

So here's to mugs that tell our truth,
With silly moments and ageless youth.
In each cup, a universe swirls,
Full of laughter, love, and twirling pearls!

Teacup Conversations

Sit with me, let's spill the tea,
Muffin crumbs and secrets flee.
Jokes about steeping, oh what a sight,
Caffeine-fueled laughter takes flight.

The kettle whistles, time for a chat,
Gossip flows faster than a cat.
Your mug is pink, mine's bright green,
We're the quirkiest duo you've ever seen.

Spilling sugar like confetti, oh dear,
Reveling in each laugh and cheer.
Tea leaves dance, swirling around,
In this cup, happiness is found.

With every sip, our thoughts take flight,
Like butterflies in fuzzy daylight.
We sip and snicker, time on freeze,
Who knew tea could bring such ease?

Beneath the Surface

Steeping tea with playful eyes,
What's hiding beneath, oh what a surprise!
Swirling thoughts and fruity zest,
Decoding flavors, we make the best.

Lemongrass whispers secrets untold,
While chamomile dreams of legends old.
Every sip's a puzzle and a tease,
What deep thoughts roam with such ease?

Plumbing depths of every brew,
Infusing laughter is our cue.
A slurp here, a giggle there,
Underneath the steam, we lay bare.

At the bottom, a leaf or two,
Wishes and giggles mix in the brew.
Who knew such depth in a simple drink?
Let's raise our cups, and not overthink!

Embracing the Ritual

Boil the water, hear it sing,
A ritual dance, dear tea we bring.
Scoops of joy and a sprinkle of fun,
Watch as the leaves do a jig and run.

Ceramic cups, like old friends in line,
Each one crafted, oh so divine.
Tea time's our break, a wacky ballet,
Sipping and savoring, come what may.

Add a splash of laughter, a spoon of cheer,
With a dash of silliness, nothing to fear.
Can you taste the joy? Can you see the light?
In our tea party world, everything's right.

Brewed moments that tickle and tease,
With every sip, we aim to please.
So here's to our cups, clinking in glee,
Our tea ritual's where we long to be!

Flavorful Journeys

Traveling cups, where will we go?
To fields of berries, or spice roads aglow?
Sip by sip, we wander and weave,
In this journey, we always believe.

Honey drips like laughter sincere,
Each flavor whispers, 'Have no fear!'
From minty hills to chocolate streams,
In every cup, we chase our dreams.

Roaming the globe with every taste,
Steeping adventures, never a waste.
Coconut shores or a ginger rush,
In our teacups, there's always a hush.

So lift your mug, let's toast our fate,
In every blend, there's something great.
Flavorful journeys through the swirl,
In this crazy world, let's give it a twirl!

Tea's Tender Touch

In my cup, a swirl of dreams,
Laughter bubbling like the streams.
Each sip's a giggle, a frothy cheer,
Whispers of joy that draw me near.

A teabag knocks and starts a fight,
"Steep me longer!" A silly sight.
I blink and grin, what's life's big plan?
Tea with a dash of humor, man!

Steam rising high, look at it dance,
Life's got rhythm, so take a chance.
A cozy blend, warm as a hug,
Steeping my worries, snug as a bug.

In every cup, a joke is steeped,
Secrets of laughter, lovingly keep.
So here's to tea, the jester bright,
In every sip, I find delight!

The Pause in Life

Kick back, my friend, it's tea-time bliss,
A moment's pause, you cannot miss.
Kettle whistles, a calls for fun,
Let's spill some laughs while we're on the run.

The cup's a stage for silly tales,
With every droplet, humor sails.
"Why the long face?" the teapot grins,
"Chill out, buddy; the fun begins!"

Sipping slowly, I see the world,
In aromatic swirls, joy is twirled.
Life's a circus, tea's the clown,
With every sip, let frowns drown down.

So raise your cup, let life uncap,
A brew of giggles in a snazzy wrap.
We pause to laugh, our spirits soar,
Tea's sweet embrace — who could want more?

Embracing Epiphanies

A teapot whispers wisdom clear,
Caffeine dreams knocking at my ear.
"Why so serious?" it nudges me,
Pour a little fun, let it be free!

Slices of lemon, a splash of zest,
Hot liquid hugs are simply the best.
In every drop, a spark of wit,
Eureka moments make me sit!

The leaves unfurl like comic strips,
Unraveling mysteries on my lips.
"Life's a jest," the teacup winks,
Sip up your giggles, don't overthink!

Delivering joy with every steep,
A swirl of laughter, no need to keep.
Epiphanies brew in laughter's hold,
With every cup, a joy retold!

Ceramics of the Spirit

A mug of my life, cracked but bright,
In its mishaps, there's pure delight.
Kintsugi gold on my clumsy heart,
Each sip a story, a delightful art.

The surface glistens, a tale does brew,
Pouring wisdom, like morning dew.
"I'm here for tea," my vessel sings,
In this chaos, joy still springs.

Spills and dribbles, a messy charm,
Comfort in chaos, it keeps me warm.
A cup rings out, chimes of hope,
In every clank, I learn to cope.

So lift your tea, embrace the fun,
Through every spill, life's colors run.
Ceramics of spirit, joyful and true,
In every sip, a chuckle anew!

www.ingramcontent.com/pod-product-compliance
Lightning Source LLC
Chambersburg PA
CBHW051629160426
43209CB00004B/570